Command Attention

Communication Techniques for Engaging Your Audience

Table of Contents

Chapter 1. Introduction

Presenting our insightful Special Report on 'Command Attention: Communication Techniques for Engaging Your Audience'. Say goodbye to dull monologues and overlooked presentations, and step into a world where your every word resonates with your audience and invites rapt attention. In this compelling report, we'll unravel powerful and efficient tactics that assure your voice is not just heard, but listened to and appreciated. Learn how to craft engaging stories, use persuasive narratives, and infuse your talk with a charm that holds your audience spellbound. Effortlessly influence, inspire and ensure your audience hangs onto your every word, every time. Intrigued? Enhance your communication prowess and transform the way the world perceives you by getting your hands on this must-read Special Report. Be the communication maestro you were always meant to be!

Chapter 2. Unlocking the Power of Verbal Communication

In our quest to become effective communicators, mastering verbal communication is paramount. It's about much more than just talking; it's an intricate mix of tone, volume, pitch, pace and the underlying sentiments. It also concerns the ability to understand and be understood—to convey clear and concise messages, sprinkled with the captivating power of storytelling. By harnessing and honing these skills, we avail ourselves of profound benefits, both in professional and personal realms.

2.1. The Essence of Verbal Communication

Understanding verbal communication at its core has less to do with the literal content of the words spoken, and more to do with the way those words are delivered. The same phrase, carried by different tones of voice, takes on completely different meanings. For example, 'Really?' can be a sign of surprise, disbelief, disappointment, or an entire gamut of other emotions—based solely on the tone with which it's spoken. It's an illuminative example of why we must focus on understanding the rudiments of verbal communication and explore how to best wield them.

When we delve deeper into verbal communication, we find a few key components that every communication maestro must recognize and use to their benefit.

1. Tone: The emotional context of your words. Your tone can dramatically alter the meaning of your utterance.

2. Volume: The strength or intensity of your voice. Your volume must be adequately used to stress important points.

3. Pace: The speed at which you speak. A fluctuating pace keeps the audience engaged and heightens the impact of your speech.

4. Pitch: The highness or lowness of your voice. It plays a critical role in maintaining interest and attention.

5. Pause: A short rest in speech adds emphasis, promotes understanding and engages the listener.

2.2. The Influence of Non-Verbal Signals

Often, we deceptively think of verbal communication as only 'spoken words', overlooking the enthralling power of non-verbal signals. Our body language, including facial expressions, gestures, eye contact, and posture, communicates as much, if not more, than the words we utter.

Our body language can betray our feelings, give weight to our words, or sabotage our message entirely, making it imperative that we're conscious of our non-verbal cues. If we claim to be open to discussion, but our arms are crossed defensively in front of us, our message is mixed. If we're speaking about a passionate subject, but our voice remains monotonous and our face expressionless, our audience may question the sincerity of our words.

One exercise that really hones our awareness of this facet is to watch recordings of effective public speakers with the volume turned off, observing their body language and expressions. Then, when rewatching with the volume restored, we can spot the alignment between verbal and non-verbal communication.

2.3. Employing Persuasive Tactics

To hold your audience's attention, your arguments and viewpoints need to be persuasive. Polishing your reasoning skills and understanding how evidence, logic, and emotion are interconnected can help in making your verbal communication highly persuasive.

Here are several proven persuasive techniques:

1. Storytelling: Sharing a relevant and engaging story can make your point more alive and personal. It stays with the listener longer than bare facts.

2. Ethos, Logos, Pathos: Build credibility (Ethos), appeal to the audience's logic (Logos) and engage their emotion (Pathos).

3. Repetition: Key points, when repeated, can become more memorable.

4. Analogies and metaphors: These can simplify complex ideas and make them relatable and understandable.

5. Power of three: Statements or ideas presented in groups of three are more satisfying and impactful for the audience.

2.4. Effective Interpersonal Communication

Being an excellent communicator doesn't merely point to oratory skills, but it also encompasses active listening and responding empathetically. Sure, your speaking skills are vital, but true communication occurs when there's an exchange of ideas, feelings, and thoughts.

Active listening is the act of engaging fully in the conversation, giving undivided attention, and providing feedback. It aims to understand the speaker's perspective, constructively respond to it, and make them feel heard.

Empathetic response, on the other hand, involves reacting to someone else's feelings with consideration and care. It bridges the gap between speakers, fosters understanding, and breeds mutual respect.

2.5. Mastering Public Speaking

A fundamental aspect of verbal communication is the ability to address a gathering effectively. Public speaking goes beyond the conference room—it includes broadcasting virtual meetings, delivering a toast at a wedding, or even pitching an idea to your boss.

Some critical points to keep in mind for effectively taking the stage are:

1. Prepare meticulously: Understand your audience, the purpose of your talk and extensively research your topic.

2. Rehearse thoroughly: Practice your speech aloud and fine-tune the elements of delivery.

3. Command your space: Use purposeful movements to appear more confident and authoritative.

4. Create visual aids: Develop engaging visuals that support what you are saying.

5. Manage your nerves: Transform your stress into positive energy that enhances your performance.

Regardless of the size of your audience, delivering a clear, engaging speaker performance can earn you a unique commanding presence that leaves a lasting impression.

In sum, whether for one-on-one conversations, team meetings, or addressing a huge crowd, being able to clearly and effectively verbally communicate is a powerful skill-set—its mastery confers a multitude of advantages in our personal and professional lives. With understanding, practice, and a willingness to improve, you too can unlock the immense potential of verbal communication. Let's embark on this journey of transforming the everyday speaker into the communication maestro you were always meant to be!

Chapter 3. Mastering Non-Verbal Cues for Effective Storytelling

First impressions are almost always created without uttering a word. When it comes to storytelling, your audience gauges your credibility and potential before you even commence your speech. Thus, non-verbal cues play a pivotal role in establishing your initial rapport and sustaining audience engagement throughout your presentation. In this section, we will delve deeper into understanding the art and science of non-verbal cues and how you can master them for effective storytelling.

3.1. Understanding Non-Verbal Cues

Non-verbal cues can be efficiently grouped into three broad categories: facial expressions, body language, and vocal tonality. Facial expressions are your emotions personified, resonating your excitement, fear, intrigue, and so forth. Body language, on the other hand, narrates the unwritten story of your confidence, comfort, sincerity, and authority. Vocal tonality breathes life into your stories, with varying pitches highlighting dramatic transitions, revelations, and conclusions.

3.2. Mastering Facial Expressions

Eyes are often branded as windows to your soul, and rightfully so. They are the most expressive component of your face and are highly capable of drawing the attention of your audience. Naturally, eye contact with your audience can spellbind them, inviting them into your narrative. Practice sincerity in your expressions to exude authenticity and make your stories more relatable.

In addition to eyes, your overall facial expressions including your smiles and frowns can make or break your story's impact. Your enthusiasm reflected in your expressions can induce excitement in your audience, while your solemnity can cast an attentive silence.

3.3. Embodying Body Language

Your posture, gestures and movements, collectively known as body language, are as impactful as your spoken words. Maintaining a confident posture with shoulders thrown back and head held high instills a sense of authority. Predominant use of open gestures, such as spreading your arms wide or showcasing your palms, radiates an aura of warmth and openness, encouraging your audience to lean in for more.

Positioning and movement in space symbolize different narrative elements. For instance, moving forward towards your listeners while making a point can emphasize the importance of what you are saying. Similarly, pacing the stage strategically can keep your audience connected and engaged.

3.4. Orchestrating Vocal Tonality

Developing a command over your vocal tonality can create mood and atmosphere, and invoke emotional responses from your audience. A steady, relaxed pace signals confidence and provides the listeners time to assimilate your story.

Our vocal sounds fluctuate based on loudness, pitch, and speed. Learning to manipulate these features can significantly amplify the effects of your storytelling. A raised volume can depict intensity or excitement, a lower pitch can signal seriousness or significance, and changing speed can generate curiosity, suspense, or revelation, depending upon the narrative.

3.5. Practice Makes Perfect

Understanding and mastering the art of non-verbal cues is not an overnight task. It demands practice and can at times even require stepping out of your comfort zone. Start with small groups and work your way up. Observe and emulate great speakers and storytellers, understanding their utilization of non-verbal cues.

3.6. Wrapping It Up

Mastering non-verbal cues is an essential aspect of engaging and persuasive storytelling. Good speakers tell a story, great speakers make the audience live that story. Your speech painted with vivid non-verbal cues can transcend ordinary storytelling, transforming your messages into experiences that your audience cherishes. Embrace these tools and embody the stories you narrate, and watch your audiences hang onto your every word, every time.

Remember that the power is in your hands – or rather, in your expressions, your body language, and your voice. Take control of these components and use them to your advantage. After all, everyone loves a good story, and your audience is no different.

Chapter 4. The Art to Captivating Audiences: The World of Storytelling

Storytelling has time and again proven to be a dynamic communication tool, able to bridge the gap between speaker and listener in a torrent of captivating anecdotes and illustrations. But, what exactly is at the root of its transcendental quality, and how can you wield it to engage your audience?

4.1. The Intricacies of Storytelling

Storytelling, at its core, is an art. It's the skill of rendering life into words - transforming mundane occurrences into captivating narratives by breathing life into characters, conjuring visual imagery and evoking profound emotions. Great storytellers have the ability to engage listeners on a cognitive, emotional, and psychological level, tapping into the power of narrative to change attitudes, beliefs, and behaviors.

The art of storytelling isn't just for novelists and playwrights. It has critical implications in the world of public speaking and communication. As a speaker, your mission is not just to relay information but to make that information compelling and impactful. Stories help you do just that.

4.2. The Mechanics of an Engaging Story

An engaging story is built just like any exquisite piece of art – meticulously crafted with precise strokes of ingenuity, authenticity, and relatability. Let's explore the anatomy of a captivating story.

- Setting: Every effective story begins with an immersive setting. It's the context for your narrative, providing the backdrop against which your story unfolds. An immersive setting paints a mental picture for your listeners, allowing them to visualize the scenario you're presenting.

- Characters: Characters are the heart of any story. When you're sharing a narrative, it's through the lens of key characters that your audience will connect. These characters could be real people, concepts, or even companies.

- Conflict: No story is complete without a conflict or a challenge. It is this friction that keeps your audience invested and engaged. It's not crucial that the conflict be dramatic, even subtle challenges can make for compelling content if presented correctly.

- Resolution: The resolution is where you tie the loose ends, present the solution to the conflict, and deliver the key message.

Remember, the effectiveness of your story in engaging your audience largely hinges upon these elements.

4.3. Storytelling for Audience Engagement

Not all stories are told the same way; they require a tailored approach depending upon the motifs, audience, and your ultimate speaking goal. Here are some tips to employ effective storytelling for audience engagement:

- Know your audience: An integral part of good storytelling is understanding your audience - their values, their anxieties, and their dreams. It will help you tailor your content to resonate with them.

- Be Authentic: Authenticity is potent. Real-life stories and experiences can create a deeper sense of connection. They make your message relatable and compelling.

- Include Sensory Details: Embellish your story with sensory details. Describe what characters saw, heard, smelled, tasted, felt – such a vivid description anchors listeners' attention.

- Clarity and simplicity: Overly complicated narratives can make it hard for your audience to follow. Make your story concise and straightforward, stripping it down to the essential elements.

- Emotional Appeal: Tap into emotions. Happiness, sadness, anticipation, or even anger can serve to engage attention and create memorable associations.

4.4. The Immense Possibilities of Storytelling in Communication

The magic of storytelling in communication is its versatility. Whether it's delivering a keynote address, giving a sales presentation, or holding a team meeting, effective storytelling can work wonders in any communicational context.

Through storytelling, complex data transforms into an engaging narrative, company goals morph into inspiring visions, and sales pitches evolve into compelling demonstrations.

Today's demanding communication landscape calls for something beyond polished phrases and factual relay. It beckons towards connection, empathy, and engagement. Storytelling, with its immense possibilities, answers that call.

By employing effective storytelling, you can create an engaging communication atmosphere where your audience is not mere spectators, but active participants in your narrative. In this echo of shared experiences and resonating messages, your communication prowess expands, and you position yourself not just as another speaker, but as a captivating weaver of tales.

In the realm of communication, storytelling is undeniably a mighty tool – a tool worth understanding, cultivating, and wielding.

As we venture into the world of storytelling, remember that practice makes perfect. Even if your storytelling skills are currently less than stellar, have faith, for just as a rough stone can be sculpted into a beautiful statue, your narrative abilities can be honed into very compelling content. Embrace the art of storytelling, and watch your public speaking transform from a monotonous transfer of information into a vibrant exchange of experiences and insights. Craft your narratives with the precision of a wordsmith, immerse your audience in your world, and leave an aftertaste of inspiration. This is the art of captivating audiences through storytelling. Welcome to a world where your voice carries the enchantment of narratives.

Chapter 5. Understanding Audience: The Key to Persuasive Communication

The first step toward becoming a master communicator is not learning how to talk, but understanding how to listen. Most importantly, that requires understanding your audience. Truly exceptional speakers are not just those who can deliver a sterling speech, but those who can fine-tune their delivery based on who they are speaking to.

5.1. Identifying Your Audience

It may sound elementary, but before you can effectively reach your audience, you must first identify them. Are they your employees, peers, or maybe clients? Knowing who will be on the receiving end of your communication is the foundation upon which your entire communication strategy should be built.

For example, if you are addressing a group of clients, your tone might be more formal, using industry jargon or specialized language. If you are speaking to employees, your tone could be relaxed, and you might use internal jargon or lingo. It's a simple point, but its implications are far-reaching.

5.2. Adopting the Right Tone

Once you've identified your audience, the next step is essential - adopting the right tone. The 'right tone' should ideally match the expectations and preferences of your audience. Corporate clients may require a more business-like and professional tone, while a younger crowd may resonate with a casual, friendly approach.

It's essential not to confuse 'tone' with 'voice.' Your voice — your brand's personality and values — should remain consistent, but your tone should shift to suit the situation. Imagine your voice as the music in a film: it sets the general mood, but the tone sets the specific feel of an individual scene.

5.3. Tailoring Your Content

Audience understanding also guides the content of your conversation. What are the interests, values, beliefs, and preferences of your audience? This information is essential as it indicates the kind of content that might resonate with them.

Updating yourself on crucial statistics or industry reports can help make your communication more effective. If you are privy to your audience's preferences, you will be in a better position to create an impactful communication strategy.

5.4. Listening to Your Audience

Effective communication is not a monologue but a dialogue. Listening, therefore, forms an essential part of any communication process. By listening to your audience, you get a vital insight into their thoughts, objections, and concerns.

Active listening, as opposed to passive listening, can provide you with deeper insights into your audience's mindset. It's about fully engaging with your audience, understanding their perspectives, and responding appropriately. This allows you to address any issues or concerns promptly, making your audience feel heard and understood, which, in turn, strengthens your connection with them.

5.5. Establishing a Connection

Establishing a genuine connection with your audience is the cornerstone of persuasive communication. Every audience wants to feel that the speaker cares about them. That connection is forged through a speaker's understanding of the audience's needs, values, and interests. By tapping into these, you can make your communication more compelling and personal.

When your audience can see their reflection in your words, they will feel understood and validated. This emotional connection is what makes communication truly effective. It not only encourages your audience to listen attentively but also to support and advocate your ideas.

Understanding your audience is a finely-honed skill that takes dedication, research, and a lot of listening. But when you truly understand your audience, you won't just have listeners — you'll have disciples. Your words will cease to be mere speech and become a personal conversation. Empathy is the key to this door.

5.6. Balancing Facts and Emotion

While understanding the audience is essential, equally important is the ability to balance facts with emotion in your communication. A successful speaker can thread the needle between sharing data and tugging at the heartstrings.

Relying solely on hard facts can make your communication dry and uninteresting. However, an over-reliance on emotion may fail to convince your audience of the trustworthiness or validity of your message. A blend of both significantly enhances your chances of delivering a compelling message.

5.7. Handling Resistance

Every informed speaker must be prepared to encounter resistance. Resistance from an audience can come in many forms, including objections, indifference, or even hostility. Understanding your audience allows you to preemptively identify likely areas of friction and plan your response.

The more you understand your audience, the better you become at managing resistance. Disarming objections with facts, empathy, and a strong narrative can earn the respect of your audience, showing that you value their opinions and concerns.

Remember, communication is not just about speaking your mind but also planting the seeds of ideas, influence, and inspiration. You can only achieve this if you comprehend your audience and their concerns, and tailor your communication to reach them effectively.

5.8. Wrapping Up

Understanding your audience is the cornerstone of persuasive communication. From identifying your audience and adopting the right tone to balancing facts and emotion, several aspects need to be considered.

In a world filled with noise, it's not enough to be heard; you need to be understood. And the only surefire way to be understood is to first understand. Understand your audience, their needs, their values, and their resistance. Then, and only then, will you truly command their attention and respect. So, tune in, listen, learn, and lead — the mantra of an extraordinary communicator.

Chapter 6. Tools for Enhancing Your Credibility and Authenticity

Credibility and authenticity are essential traits to foster for anyone striving for effective communication. They establish trust, encourage dialogue, and foster a genuine connection with your audience. Harnessing tools to enhance these attributes can transform your communication game and give your voice the power to command attention effortlessly. So, let's dive in and explore these tools in detail.

6.1. Understanding Credibility

Credibility is the perceived authenticity and trustworthiness that you project to your audience. This image is built over time through consistent behaviour, honesty, expertise, and your ability to meet commitments.

The first tool to bolster your credibility is demonstrating your expertise and knowledge in your chosen field. If your audience believes you're an expert, they are more likely to trust your words and opinions. To project expertise, it is crucial to stay abreast with industry trends, ground-breaking research, and latest developments. After all, knowledge is power.

Another important aspect of credibility is integrity. People trust those who "walk the talk". Your actions should be consistent with your words. If you promise to deliver a report by Friday, ensure that it is done. If you commit to a meeting at a certain time, make sure you aren't late.

Transparency is also key to building credibility. Avoiding half-truths and deceptive practices will prevent eroding trust. When mistakes happen, own up to them rather than diverting the blame.

6.2. Enhancing Authenticity

Being authentic means being true to who you are – your thoughts, your values, and your style. It is about presenting your genuine self to your audience, free from pretense and affectation.

The first step towards authenticity is self-awareness. Understand your strengths, weaknesses, and values. Reflect on what drives you and how it affects your communication style. This introspection will help you align your actions with your true self, making your authenticity apparent to your audience.

Authentic communicators also exhibit empathy. They tune into their audience's emotions and thoughts, responding and adapting their message accordingly. Convey your understanding and care for their needs and concerns, and your audience will reciprocate with trust and loyalty.

Being open is another hallmark of authenticity. Don't be afraid to share your thoughts and feelings - including your vulnerabilities. Paradoxically, vulnerability often strengthens the bond between the speaker and the listener, as it reveals the speaker's humanity and fosters connection on a deeper level.

Lastly, consistency in your behaviour and communication completes the authenticity circle. Inconsistency can project inauthenticity and damage trust. Ensure your actions and words reflect your personality and values consistently – be the same person in every situation.

6.3. Leveraging Verbal Tools

Your voice can be your powerful ally in communicating credibility and authenticity. Here's how to use it effectively.

Choosing the right words is important. Avoid jargon or overly complex language that can confuse or alienate your audience. Use language that connects with your audience, is easy to understand and helps you express your genuine sentiments.

Your tone of voice also plays a crucial role. A monotone voice can come off as disinterested or robotic. Conversely, a lively, passionate, and expressive tone connects better with listeners and reflects your excitement and dedication to the topic.

Speaking speed is another factor. Speak too quickly, you appear nervous or rushed; too slowly, you risk losing the audience's attention. Aim for a balance that allows your audience to absorb your message comfortably.

6.4. Utilizing Non-Verbal Tools

Non-verbal communication plays a pivotal role in projecting authenticity and credibility.

Body language can speak volumes about your confidence. Standing upright, maintaining eye contact, using open postures, and avoiding fidgeting communicates credibility and self-assurance. Mirroring your audience's body language can create a bond and indicate empathy.

Facial expressions are equally important. Your face often reveals your genuine emotions. A sincere smile can project warmth and friendliness, while a serious expression can convey dedication and concern for a topic.

Lastly, practicing active listening signals respect and engagement with your audience. By nodding, rephrasing, or asking relevant questions, your audience feels heard and validated, increasing your credibility and authenticity.

To sum up, enhancing credibility and authenticity can revolutionize your communication game. It takes time and consistent effort, but before you know it, you'll command attention effortlessly, captivate audiences, and make a lasting impression.

Chapter 7. Nailing the First Impressions: Strategies for Commanding Attention

When it comes to communication, first impressions are monumental. They establish the tone and set expectations, serving as your audience's opening glance into who you are and what you're about. Thus, commanding attention from the onset is critical. It lays a sturdy foundation for the persuasiveness and authenticity of the rest of your message. In this chapter, we explore a plethora of thoughtful tactics designed to help you nail those precious initial moments.

7.1. Know Your Audience

Understanding your audience is the first stepping stone. Collecting insights and analyzing their needs, interests, and perspectives can guide you in framing an appropriate, engaging introduction. Knowing the demographic facts, their background related to your topic, and their expectations can spark connections right off the bat.

7.2. Prepare Yourself

Proper preparation saves people from poor performances. Allocate adequate time and effort towards planning, organizing, and crafting your initial statements, understanding that they will shape the ambience of the rest of your presentation. Ensure your preparation extends beyond content. Wear confidence-inspiring attire, work on your body language, and practice your delivery.

7.3. Perfect Your Elevator Pitch

In many communications, you are your own product. Therefore, being able to communicate who you are and what you do succinctly can be extremely advantageous. An elevator pitch is a roughly 30 second to 2 minute response to the age-old prompt, "Tell me about yourself." It provides context and helps your audience understand your relevance. Remember that an elevator pitch isn't a sales pitch, but rather a brief, compelling speech that sparks curiosity about your personal or professional offerings.

7.4. Capitalize on Your Non-Verbal Cues

Our non-verbal cues can speak louder than our verbal communication. Pay attention to facial expressions, hand gestures, body alignment, and eye contact. Maintain an upright, friendly, open posture and a pleasing facial expression. These action signals are a critical part of nailing your first impression.

7.5. Ensure a Purposeful Opening

A powerful opening captivates your audience's attention. You can start with an intriguing question, an unusual fact, a captivating story or throw in some humor. This variety helps you connect to your audience emotionally and intellectually.

7.6. Make it Interactive

An interactive start can be effective in breaking the ice. Ask your audience questions to encourage their participation or conduct a quick poll to measure their views on a topic. This engagement increases the chance your audience will pay attention throughout your communication because they feel integrally involved.

7.7. The Importance of Authenticity

In an era where authenticity is increasingly valued, being your true self can immediately command attention. Allow your audience to see your human side. Share your challenges, your victories, and your vantage point. This creates a level of trust and rapport between you and your audience.

7.8. Practice Active Listening

Active listening entails giving your full attention and responding in a manner that shows understanding during a dialogue. People are more likely to listen to and respect those who display responsive, empathetic listening behaviors. By showing your regard for others' perspectives, the mutual respect fosters increased attention in future dialogue.

7.9. Leverage assertiveness and enthusiasm

Assertiveness emphasizes standing for your beliefs and expressing your thoughts, feelings, and needs in a direct, honest, and appropriate way. Precise assertiveness helps your audience appreciate your confidence and trust your message. Meanwhile, enthusiasm injects energy into your communication, helps hold attention, and makes your presentation memorable.

In summary, you can nail your first impressions and command attention by employing a blend of these meticulously curated strategies. By understanding your audience's needs, you can craft a purposeful opening and engage them in interactive dialogue. Demonstrating authenticity and enthusiasm alongside strong, non-verbal cues, and active listening will ensure your audience is hooked right from the start. These strategies will not only draw attention but also create an impactful, lasting impression.

Chapter 8. Rhetorical Techniques to Amp Up Your Talks

Rhetoric is a fusion of both art and science. As an art, it empowers speakers to charm, persuade, and inspire their audience through the careful usage of language. As a science, it rigorously scrutinizes and builds upon established techniques to improve communication. Being cognizant of these techniques not just enhances your speeches but elevates them to the level of art. With these tools, you can sculpt your speech to command the attention of your audience, play with their emotions, and prompt them to act.

8.1. The Power of Analogies

Analogies are phenomenal rhetorical devices that can add a layer of richness and interest to your communication. They permit a speaker to transfer the meaning or familiarity from one concept to the other. In a way, analogies create a mental bridge that assists your audience in understanding complex ideas. When used well, they are a powerful tool to evoke imagination and stimulate thought in listeners' minds.

To use analogies effectively, however, you need to keep two key points in mind. Firstly, the two concepts you link shouldn't be too drastically different as it could confuse your audience instead of enlightening them. Ensure there's a degree of similarity or relatability between them. Secondly, the analogy must be relevant and should aid in understanding the message you're attempting to pass across. A misplaced analogy might only serve to distract your audience from the core message you wish to communicate.

8.2. The Art of Repetition

Repetition is a classic rhetorical technique with a dual purpose: emphasis and reinforcement. By repeating specific phrases or ideas, you nail the point within your audience's minds. It can also be a powerful tool to instill emotions, build rhythm, and create a memorable imprint of your speech.

One significant example of the use of repetition is Martin Luther King Jr.'s famous "I Have a Dream" speech. He repeats the phrase "I have a dream" to emphasize his vision for an inclusive and equal society, thus creating a lasting impression.

Implement repetition with caution. Too much repetition can dull your message or irritate your audience. Instead, use this technique sparingly and strategically to accentuate your important points.

8.3. The Magic of Triads

A triad, or a "rule of three," is another effective rhetorical technique. It involves presenting a trio of ideas or phrases in quick succession. This structure is potent because it's simple, satisfying, and memorable. It also gives a sense of completeness to your message.

Steve Jobs was a master in implementing triads. In his 2007 iPhone launch, he described it as "an iPod, a phone, and an internet communicator." This simple, rhythmic triad enabled the audience to grasp the concept of what would become a revolutionary device.

When you employ triads in your speech, carefully select three relevant points or ideas. Remember, these points should be strong enough to stand alone but together should offer a complete, cogent argument or principle.

8.4. Power of Rhetorical Questions

Rhetorical questions are a powerful tool to stimulate thought and engage your audience. In nature, they don't require an answer; instead, they aid in provoking thought or emphasizing a point. Varied in forms, rhetorical questions can be used to challenge assumptions, provoke curiosity, or declare an obvious answer.

If you ask, "Can we afford to lose our planet?" you're compelling your audience to reflect on the urgency of the subject. You're compelling them to engage with your talk and be part of it.

However, the usage of rhetorical questions should also be carefully moderated. Overuse may turn it into an irritable gimmick rather than an effective engagement tool.

Mastering these rhetorical techniques adds an additional dimension to your speeches. When carefully implemented, they can help you enthuse, engage, and convince your audience in unimaginable ways. Remember, true communication is an art where you not only deliver your ideas but also elicit emotional responses, persuade audiences, and leave lasting impressions. So, use these techniques wisely and watch the impact they have on your audience, making them hang onto your every word.

Chapter 9. Say It With Impact: The Science of Effective Presentation

Communication is integral to how we convey our thoughts, ideas, and beliefs. Effective delivery can make the difference between mere talking and impactful presenting. In this segment, we focus on the science behind persuasive presentations. We delve into keys to successful speaking strategies and unravel rhetorical tools that can exponentially increase the impact of your message.

9.1. The Backbone of Your Presentation: Structuring Your Talk

Before you begin putting pen to paper, it is crucial to understand what a well-structured presentation looks like. Respect the intelligence of your audience by crafting a narrative arc that builds, engages and finally, satisfies. A properly structured presentation comprises three main components:

1. Introduction: This is your opportunity to capture the audience's attention. A strong starting point can be a striking statement, pertinent question, startling facts or even a short anecdote. Remember to introduce the topic and the purpose of the presentation.

2. The main body: This is where you dive into the heart of the matter. Each point or sub-argument you make should follow a logical sequence resulting in an understandable and engaging narrative.

3. Conclusion: Here, you cement your argument by summarizing your main points and presenting a strong closing statement. Try

to end on a high note. It could be a call to action, or a powerful closing line that leaves a lasting impression.

9.2. Engaging the Senses: The Power of Visual Aids

Any form of visual representation, whether it's a graph, table, chart, or image can greatly enhance your overall delivery. Human brains process visual information much faster than textual data. Make sure your visual aids compliment your message and aren't overwhelming or confusing.

1. Use clear and relevant images: Avoid overly complicated or irrelevant graphics.

2. Make sure text is legible: If you include text, make sure it's large enough to read and doesn't contain complicated jargon.

3. Don't overcrowd your slides: Keep it simple. Don't try to fit everything on one slide. Distribute your content evenly.

4. Use colors wisely: Colors can invoke emotional responses. Use them smartly to highlight and differentiate between different sections or points.

9.3. Mastering Non-verbal Communication

It's not just about what you say; it's also how you say it. Non-ver—bal communication during a presentation makes a significant impact.

1. Eye contact: Make deliberate eye contact with your audience. It helps engage them and makes your communication more personal.

2. Body language: Stand tall and open. Conservative positions might

imply lack of confidence. Be mindful of your posture, hand gestures and facial expressions.

3. Vocal intonation: Your vocal pitch, volume, rate and quality play a significant role in how your message is received. Monotonous speaking patterns can disengage your audience.

4. Move around the stage: If possible, move around the stage or room. This gives an impression of confidence and control.

9.4. The Art of Storytelling in Presentations

Incorporating a narrative into your presentation keeps your audience intrigued. Stories add a human touch to facts and data, making them more resonant.

1. Keep it relevant: The story must align with the theme of your presentation.

2. Engage with emotions: Storytelling allows you to appeal to the emotional side of your audience. But remember, it's important to balance emotion with reason.

3. Call back: Referring back to your story at the end of the presentation can have a profound impact.

4. Keep it brief and engaging: Ensure your story is concise and works as a tool to drive your key points home, not a diversion.

9.5. Practice and Preparation: The Path to Confidence

Proper preparation and practice can significantly reduce anxiety. Here are some techniques:

1. Rehearse your presentation: This helps you familiarize yourself

with the content, improve your flow, and exposes areas for improvement.

2. Record and review: Recording your presentation lets you observe your non-verbal cues.

3. Seek Feedback: Practice in front of a friend, colleague or mentor to get constructive criticism.

4. Visualize a positive outcome: This can help alleviate stress and boost your confidence.

The science of effective presentation may seem complicated initially, but with understanding, practice, and persistence, it becomes second nature. Adopt these strategies and watch your communication skills evolve to new heights. Effective presentation is an art worth mastering; it has direct impacts on your personal development, career progression, and leadership skills.

Chapter 10. Working the Room: Techniques for Engaging Large Audiences

Understanding and effectively engaging a large audience can often pose a significant challenge. The essence of successful communication not only lies in the message you deliver but also in the way you deliver it. This section will dive into an exhaustive exploration of the various techniques that can aid you in arresting the attention of large audiences and keeping them actively engaged throughout your discourse.

10.1. Cultivate a Masterful Presence

Successful speakers immerse themselves in the dynamics of the room. They exude a natural aura that instantly captivates the audience. Establishing such a masterful presence involves paying attention to factors such as your body language, tone of voice, and eye contact.

Body language plays a crucial role in the perceived credibility of a speaker. To command attention, ensure your posture exudes confidence. Stand tall, with shoulders back and chest out. Make purposeful movements rather than jittery gestures, which can distract the audience or dilute your message.

Equally important is the tone of your voice. It should reverberate confidence and authority, sustaining the audience's interest. Variation in pitch, speed, volume, and tone can make your speech more engaging and less monotonous.

Another critical aspect of establishing a commanding presence is maintaining eye contact with your audience. It helps foster a connection, encourages participation, and makes your words more believable.

10.2. Develop a Connection

Commanding the room is not merely about drawing attention towards yourself. It's about fostering a sincere connection with your audience. This involves understanding who your audience is, their expectations, their challenges and presenting your message in a way that resonates with them.

Get to know your audience. You could conduct pre-event surveys or make use of shared experiences or narratives to understand their underlying needs and concerns. Adjust your message where possible to address these points. Relatability triggers interest and ultimately leads to engagement.

Use the power of stories and anecdotes, making them relevant to the audience's context. The audience is more likely to remember and empathize with a captivating story, making your message more impactful.

Also, begin sessions with a powerful opener. It could be a provocative statement, riveting statistics, or a personal story that stirs curiosity or an emotional response. Remember, an engaging start sets the tone for the rest of your talk and grabs audience attention.

10.3. Foster Interactive Communication

Interaction is a potent tool to engage large audiences. Studies indicate that an audience's attention span dwindles after 10 minutes of a monologue. By including various interactive elements in your talk, you can keep the audience alert, interested, and actively participating.

Consider incorporating Q&A sessions in between your talk instead of reserving it for the end. This not only breaks the monotony but also invites immediate clarification, encouraging active listening, and maintaining audience engagement.

Involve the audience in your discourse by asking for their opinions or conducting quick polls. Immediate feedback offers a sense of shared ownership of the conversation. Integrating technological tools like live polling or interactive presentation software can further facilitate this engagement.

10.4. Use Visual Aids Effectively

Visual aids can significantly enhance the reach and impact of your message, making it more digestible and memorable. When executed right, they can become a powerful tool for sustaining audience interest.

Ensure your slides are visually appealing and not cluttered. Use meaningful graphics and statistics to underline your point. But remember, visuals should aid your talk and not become the talk.

Incorporate short videos or demonstrations to illustrate complex concepts. This breaks the monotony, maintains interest and aids in better comprehension.

10.5. The Power of Pauses

Finally, yet importantly, do not underestimate the power of well-placed pauses. It allows your audience to digest the information, think and reflect. Strategic silence often carries more weight than torrential speech. By mastering the power of pauses, you can make your words resonate more powerfully with your listeners.

To wrap up, mastering the room doesn't mean fitting into a specific mold. Authenticity fosters connection, which ultimately is the key to command attention. By embodying these techniques, you can become the memorable speaker that leaves a lasting impact on large audiences.

Chapter 11. Closing Remarks: Leaving a Lasting Impact

The genesis of any lasting impression is the eloquence and poise with which you conclude your presentation or speech. Here, we amalgamate an array of pivotal tips and techniques to help you model a closing that not only reinforces your key message, but also leaves a compelling imprint on your audience.

11.1. Begin with Recap

A potent technique to ensure your audience retains your message is to provide a quick recap. Restate the key points you have discussed throughout your presentation. But remember, your closing should not sound like a monotonous grocery list. Weave your key points into a coherent, succinct narrative that echoes your central message.

```
*Articulate your key points in a concise, compelling
manner.
*Create a narrative that binds your core ideas together.
*Use language that is simple to understand yet powerful
in leaving an impression.
*Avoid information overload. Selectively choose points
to reiterate.
```

11.2. Reiterate Your Purpose

In the vein of restating key points, do not forget to reinstate the purpose of your presentation or speech. This gives your audience a clear takeaway and guiderails to interpret your message. Remind them why the information you imparted is of value, and how it ties into the larger context of their work or lives.

> *Highlight the purpose behind your presentation; the 'why' behind the 'what'.
> *Describe how the key points align with this purpose.
> *Explain what your audience stands to gain by embracing your message.
> *Create a final vision around your purpose to make it more captivating.

11.3. Use a Powerful Quotation

A compelling quotation that aligns with your message can be an effective tool in carving a lasting impact. It infuses your closing remarks with a whiff of wisdom, making it more memorable. Ensure though, that the quote you use isn't cliched, and resonates with your audience on an intellectual as well as emotional level.

> *Select a quote that ties into your central message.
> *Avoid cliched or overused quotes.
> *Choose quotes that will resonate with your audience and their experiences.

11.4. Create a Powerful Visual

People respond strongly to visuals — a moving picture or poignant image that ties into your message can enhance recall and elevate your closing remarks' impact. It could be an evocative image, an enlightening infographic or even a short video clip.

> *Choose visuals that complement your key message.
> *Ensure visuals are high-quality and clearly discernible.
> *Avoid deploying visuals just for the sake of it. They

must hold meaning and add to your narrative.

11.5. Invoke Emotion

Creating an emotional connection with your audience will make your message more memorable. By tapping into their feelings, you ensure that the memory of your presentation is charged with emotions, thus making it difficult to forget.

*Invoke emotion through personal stories or anecdotes.
*Use expressive language to trigger emotional responses.
*Strike a balance do not emotionally overwhelm your audience or sound ingenuine.

11.6. Include a Call to Action

Every impactful presentation or speech seeks to inspire an action. A potent call to action provides your audience with a clear path forward and encourages them to apply what they have learned. The call-to-action can be tangible, like reading a book or visiting a website, or intangible, like adopting a new mindset.

*Stay clear and compelling with your call to action.
*Align the call-to-action with your overall purpose.
*Make your call-to-action feasible - avoid suggesting unrealistic actions.

11.7. Engage With a Powerful Closing Line

Your final sentence is your last shot at captivating your audience, so make it count. Whether you choose to close with a rhetorical question that probes your audience's thought, a succinct summation of your central thesis, a striking assertion, or a forward-looking statement, ensure it leaves a resounding impact.

*Choose a closing line that aligns with your key points and overall purpose.
*Avoid using generic or cliched closing lines.
*Keep it concise yet impactful.
*Stoke interest, generate curiosity or inspire contemplation with your closing line.

In conclusion, a presentation's ending is an opportunity to etch your message into your audience's memory. Properly employed, these closing techniques can guide your audience toward the action you wish them to take and ensure that your message rings in their minds long after you've concluded. Remember, the closing remarks of your presentation are your parting words and these hold the power to leave an indelible impact. So, choose them with extreme care and deliberation.

www.ingramcontent.com/pod-product-compliance
Lightning Source LLC
Chambersburg PA
CBHW071013260726
48661CB00007B/2936